Wide Sk[ies]
and Bes[t] [Bitter]

Peter Phillips

To dear Hylda
With warm wishes,
Peter
Nov 05

Hearing Eye

Published by Hearing Eye

Hearing Eye
Box 1, 99 Torriano Avenue
London NW5 2RX, UK
email: books@hearingeye.org
www.hearingeye.org

Acknowledgements
Some of these poems, or versions of them, first appeared in: *Ambit, Brittle Star,
Envoi, Frogmore Papers, In The Company of Poets* (Hearing Eye), *Iota, Magma,
Other Poetry, Poetry Nottingham International, Rialto, Seam, Smiths Knoll,
The Interpreters House, The Shop, Thumbscrew, Weyfarers.*

Also by Peter Phillips from Hearing Eye:

Frayed At the Edges

Looking For You

This publication has been made possible with
the financial support of Arts Council England

Printed and bound by Cambridge University Press
Designed by Martin Parker at silbercow.co.uk

Cover photograph by the author: beach at Hunstanton

Contents

NORFOLK SCENES

1

2

3

I WANT TO BE BURIED IN A RESTAURANT

INHERITANCE

FIVE FOXES

TROUBLES AND CONTENTMENTS

In memory of Linda Phillips
and for my family

Reeds at Brancaster Staithe

If I believed in ghosts
this is where I would find them, crouched
close to pale waterways,

in reeds darkened by mud and water,
a glow of golden straw where they reach
for warmth in the salty air.

Only the marsh harriers would glimpse
them as they screeched overhead
in a tumble of earthward plunges.

Quicksilver sea grumbles into the staithe,
nudges the hull of a row-boat,
its paint old and peeled.

Clouds smudge the sky. I hear
the rustle of reeds, a whispered
conversation between lovers,
tremulous, coming in on the wind.

Mist on the Coastal Path

Mist blew in from the sea, curled
over the marshes like white muslin
ghosting the air.
We walked east out of Wells
past old whelk houses along the coastal path.

Wet light lay on hedgerows. Five dogs plunged
out of the fields —
three Labradors (two black, one golden),
two Springer Spaniels. They rushed
through us, their coats
a stream of watery fur.

I said to the man puffing up behind,
            "Are you a dog walker?"
— sometimes words just fall out.
He laughed, said they were working dogs,
he'd bred them all —
and where was my home?
"London," I said and we waved good-bye.

Slowly the mist was lifting.
He followed his dogs into the afternoon.

Norfolk Birds

Snowflakes shimmy in the breeze
as out of the fields they giggle,
heads bobbing: a party of pheasants
chattering as they cross the track.

They scurry away, a clutch
of Norfolk girls, wobbly, going home
after a night's drinking.

Then wind whisks the snow;
the birds rise over the hedgerow
into a whirling Burnham sky.

Norfolk Lads

Wearing white collars, red cravats, Harris tweed
jackets, they strut from behind a tree, scuff up

leaves in the afternoon, look a bit foppish
mincing about. Then heads poke forward

like pitchforks, they attack till one gives way,
scuttles into the memory of a hedge. Leaves

flutter, fall quiet like a tranquil pool,
until an evening shiver wakes them up again.

Walsingham Snowdrops

An oyster shell sky,
mixture of uncomfortable shadows,
light and difficulty.

As we walk through the woods, white
tablecloths of snowdrops drape
the ground, brighten our path.

It's difficult to argue
treading through so many flowers.

Cliffs at Hunstanton

The rain a fine spray
rinses out sheets of gloom
till drowned daylight drips into sleep.

Next morning on the cliff's
shoulders, there's a smell
of sea and dampness and in

it comes again, a shoal of rain,
almost a mist, like a worry
I hope will pass over.

Cakes at Sheringham Park

Around every corner flash fires of light,
shadows of colour printed on paths.

But I don't smell the rhododendrons,
their huge bell flowers tolling in the breeze.

What I see are strawberry and raspberry tarts,
apricot flans and creamy cheesecake.

I breathe in, taste the colours,
go in search of a cup of tea.

April on Holkham Beach

A flare of primroses,
pale light moving out
over sand dunes to the sea,

no clouds
just a blaze of lemon
marrying heat and breeze.

Waves tremble, a decision
being made, way off business
of tide returning to land.

When I look up
the primroses are overhead
asking to be picked.

Coastal Light

This morning in June, I walk under clouds
of thin milk, look out over mud

and slosh of marshes, past the lifeboat station
to where confidence turns to worry and sea

merges with sky. Air is warm on my arms,
sun shines and clouds become fresh linen,

a new made bed, its sheets folded back –
and here come the gulls, restless as ever.

They shoot around, and for a moment I want
them to take me up in their flight, high

into the coastal light, carry me above the shoreline.
I'll see the pier at Cromer on one side and Hunstanton

to the west with its flashy fields of lavender;
and spread in between, the burn of poppies –

Norfolk's flame, blazing hope. The gulls descend
in a squawk, off-key saxophonists yelping their music.

Then the clouds form a clearing. A glade
of blue appears. The light can't be blue, but feels it.

Road Casualties

On the B1065,
oik in an anorak —
crow feeding on a field mouse.

Then a rabbit, Peter Rabbit of my childhood
crushed like a soft toy,
tail of snow, eyes open to the sky.

Later a fox, ego crumpled on the tarmac.
Oh fox, dear fox, chancer
of your car-salesman world.
Why were you not quick enough?

At the edge of the verge, a cock pheasant,
weight knocked out.
He lies in his bundle of feathers,
too slow, too late.

In a cut cornfield: hare —
daft comedian, magician.
Tell me a joke, dance a jig.
But where are you? Gone.
Gawky legs kicking gold dust
into Norfolk's never never land,
bounding under a yellow blanket of cloud.

Don't get dead hare, don't get dead.

Rigsby in Wells-Next-the-Sea

Here it comes, my Mr Rigsby-meets-Miss Jones smile,
the one when he hopes he'll get his hands on her,
the smile which goes on forever.

The sky is a slate roof.
Charcoal sea swirls into the harbour,
so I'm wrapped in dark thoughts.

I don't like grey, but surrounded by the rush
of it, I feel the pleasure of night-time imagination
as it whisks through me.

I look for the swans,
their feathered light in the darkness,
but they are gone – only
the half-gleam of water as it floods in.

The smell of a late fry calls me
to the vinegar fluorescence of French's fish shop
and a half portion of chips.
Eating them
I feel even more Rigsby than Rigsby.

Dog Talk

What a treat for a dog from Bethnal Green:
scenting rabbit and pheasant in grass,
chase across sand into the bowl of the sea.
Sky wrapped round
the beach, a rain-wall falling
from clouds large as parks.
I'm jumping, just jumping.

Last night I lay in the sky's lap,
looked into darkness,
felt the moon cool on my back.
A collar of stars dimmed, disappeared
as the sun rolled into morning.
Far off I heard the boats unload.
The air was tangy with fish.

Then I thought of London: Victoria Park,
voices from bagel shops, curry houses,
secretary girls tickling my chin,
and the noise. It's strange,
I miss the noise.

Hog Roast on the Buttlands

There he is, H.V. Graves, the butcher.
My eyes leap 50 metres,
can already see the roast
laid out, its crunchy crackling
a steam of golden heat.

"You know this is bloody wonderful," I say
when I arrive panting.
"It's better than bloody wonderful," he says,
"and better than a woman."

"Yes, and you can put apple sauce on a roast,
can't you?" I say.
"Aye," he says, "but you can slap it
on a woman as well."

Kiss Me Quick at Wells-Next-the-Sea

I hover happy in a sweet shop,
buy a bag of chocolate raisins,
honeycomb, a Mr Whippy with a flake,
a bottle of fruity, fizzy pop;

then walk to where some crabs
are dressed for tea, a stall
with cockles, whelks and lobster.
I stand entranced, think perhaps

I'll buy some prawns with sauce,
a small pot, in case the wife comes checking
what I'm eating and if she asks,
have I been good, I'll say, "Of course!"

I left her horizontal in the sun
so I'll trust my luck,
tuck into prawns, enjoy myself
legs dangling from the quay, run

back before she wakes… but no, I think
I'll have a hot dog lashed with onions,
a pint of beer, stagger home, give
the wife a kiss, then have another drink.

Reaching for the Moon

Tonight is hot.
Low in the sky the moon
is a sliver of mango.
If I stand on tip-toe,
reach and have it for myself,
will you tell me I'm greedy?

Horse

Grey horse standing in a field
what is your name?

As I stare I feel your heat
warm under my palm.

Look at me horse.
Blow me a kiss.

Talking to Ducks

This morning silt runs into the quay.
Ducks paddle through it,
then waltzing the water
a troupe of swans.

I want to jump in,
but the sea is cold
and I don't have my water wings.
So I send out thoughts, "Come here
ducks, come here swans,
have some bread, it's nice and fresh."

They don't seem to hear me, beaks
in the sky, not looking
at the silly man waving his arms.

Perhaps the swans have Tchaikovsky in their heads
and the ducks are wondering
why they're never asked to dance,
but as they glide past, one turns,
drifts to the quay,
blinks her chocolate drop eyes,
as if she understands me.

High Tide

The white blouse of the sky opens
and rain falls,
not a raid of rain
just a silk scarf slipping to the ground.

At Blakeney quay
the tide rises towards the brim.
I hope it will flow over,
flood my feet.

Out in the bay, seals dive
into the green hole of the sea, enjoy
the hug of autumn's wind,
an ice pack on their shoulders.

Boats are anchored. Their masts, bare
of sails, prick the empty skyline privacy
of my thoughts.

There's a companionship here
of time and weather,
a falling back in years...

until the sea spills over,
leaves me feet-wet and smiling
as the sky does up her buttons.

Seals at Blakeney

If I were a seal
silvery-grey with long whiskers,
I'd gulp fish straight down my throat,
turn cartwheels, show off
to those sideway crabs, creepy lobsters.

If any sightseers came near
I'd jump on them,
take them out to the Point
to swim with the skate.

I want to be a common seal,
to lounge on thighs of sand,
breasts of dunes, peer
at excited tourists, my head
just above the wash of waves.

A Pink Sun is Falling

and behind scruffy hedgerows
it turns evening stubble to gold
as shadows light the ground.

It's as if the face of an old man
has been lit up; one moment
he's a worry of himself,
then a smile.

I look again. The sun disappears.
Sky glooms
and the field becomes a frown.

Victoria Sponge on the Buttlands

Ladies of the W.I. flutter amongst
a population of cakes
and sitting in state is their monarch,
a Victoria sponge,
the ermine of her fresh cream
spread all around.

"I must have that for tea," I think,
and as I fumble for some coins
I see the cake's procession into another's hands.

"But, but…" I mutter, "I'd like that."
Father would have been quicker,
had his money out,
already grabbed it from its throne.

I scuff the ground, I'm like a spoilt fox,
not hungry but still want to eat.
Two pigeons bob past me –
shall I kick them?
No, they seem happy and in love,
but they've not lost a delicious cream cake.

And here's my wife,
the one who saves me from myself,
with a smile as tempting
as any Victoria sponge.
"Come here," she says "It's tea time."

Dusk

Light's nearly gone, dissolving
like drizzle in a memory of shadows.

Tide fills the quay and damp air
is a silver gloss on the water.

I look to where the marshes sprawl,
see a buoy blink its green light,

hold my face to the rain,
lick Norfolk from my lips. A gust

of gulls blows everywhere. Limes
on the Buttlands are a twist

of tangled branches. The black tent of the sky
goes up and they disappear into darkness.

Cows at Hunworth

Cows lollop in the river,
trail past like philosophers
learned in the truth of cows.

Some bathe in the water,
luxuriate under an oak tree,
its trunk stooped to give them shade.

I wonder if they have a favourite cow,
a friend to moo to
about aching hooves and sore udders,
or in their milky world of pasture
is grass their only real friend?

They squelch up the bank, chew sun
from the field. I want to touch, rest
my face on the warm meadow of their backs,
hear the rumble of their thoughts,
stand in solidarity and peace.

But they're soon gone —
a cloud of cows in the gentle breeze.

I Love Norfolk Grass

I could eat plates of it.

For starters, new grass mixed with samphire,
poppy petals and buttercups;
a main course of long grass sprinkled
with cornflowers, daisies
and a dash of mustard dressing.
Then I'd ask for a savoury dish,
rough grass and a poached egg on top
salted with Cromer sea spray, garnished
with a four-leaf clover.

When offered a drink,
I'd say no to grass juice,
ask for a lager instead.

What do you think I am, a horse?

Hoste Arms, Burnham Market

Here Chelsea greets her Norfolk cousin,
BMW meets Range Rover,
black boots become green wellies.

The Hoste Arms is theatre, its restaurant
the stage: lights down, curtain up.

Enter businessman talking FT index,
international markets. He strides to his table,
knocks back Brancaster oysters, looks forward
to a fishy night with his secretary.

Up through a trap door,
a toff in crimson trousers
talks as if he owns the county,
and most likely does.
Sea bass swims to his table.

Weekend couple swing in from the wings,
glug back Chilean chardonnay.
He's Steak and Chips. She's Mrs Cod.

Spotlight over family folk:
they wear jeans, T-shirts and trainers,
sit up straight,

behave like mother's watching,
and she is.

11pm. The cast takes a bow.
The chap in the corner with a Stella,
review written, closes his notebook.

Wide Skies, Salt and Best Bitter

Wood smoke in the night,
burn of old oak,
years smouldering into wide skies.

Cold hands want burning logs,
cheeks the fire's blush,
but smoke whispering along Staithe Street
will have to be enough.

Sea is at full tide,
its surface gloss a flowing quilt,
ironed, ready to draw back.

Salt blends with smoky air.
I breathe the flush of the moment –
it trickles down like a pint of beer.

I turn onto the Buttlands, walk
to the Globe and on past the Crown.
Everywhere the sound of drink,
but I've had mine already,
best bitter still on my breath.

Sheep at Holkham

I stand on the beach. All that can be heard
is quiet traffic of waves. Sea comes in,

wipes my footprints from the sand. As I walk
through pine trees, cold air hoofs past me

towards sheep feeding on a winter scrub of grass.
Night spreads its dark sheet over the ground;

sheep are bundled into twos and threes.
I want to hug their contentedness, feel

the baa-lamb calm of their warmth, enjoy days
just chewing. But is it fair to fling myself at them,

spoil their night's sleep, bring dysfunction into their lives?
The drone of the sea is their distant comfort.

The Deer

Threadbare sheets spread
over the land, thin shadows
falling to the ground.

Edged from the scruff of the forest,
a deer raises her head, sniffs the silence,
listens again to the quiet,
strides out of the trees,
model girl on a catwalk.

I screw my eyes, see a man lean forward,
hesitate against sallow air, his feet
lost in worried furrows of the field.
His gun follows the deer, traces
the geometry of her legs, back and neck.

He fires. His gun jerks skywards.
She drops,
he blows into his hands
breaks open his gun and goes on.

Later, sipping his beer,
he peers into the sky of its pale head,
drinks it down, licks his lips.

Seagulls, Morston

The sea's cold face chills the air;
gulls quiver about, edgy
whether to land on the quay or water
as if they'd like to float
on the tide but are wary
of getting wet. They fly upwards,
dodge between each other
in moments of grace and awkwardness.

I feel the close shave of the wind:
its old blade chafes my cheeks
with a glow of cold.
I stare over the creek
watch squads of waves battle
inland, capture the marsh.

Now the sky is losing daylight,
shadows are thinner.
A swoop of gulls lands nearby,
tired and spent, like lovers.

Wild Spirits

I stood on mudflats still clammy
with the taste of tide.
The land was a pencil drawing
empty of colour: fields, trees
and an afternoon sky drained of ambition.

Then the geese appeared.

I felt low hunger,
watched wings flap and swoop
from distant reeds in the weak Norfolk air.

I saw them circle, test wind-speed, direction
and light, arc a triumphant loop,
fly east, leaving a trail of thoughts
as they shot past,
wild spirits in formation
towards new continents
and a stronger sky.

Limes on the Buttlands

Snow fell in the night, a silent
sleep of it. Lime trees, old and gnarled,
surround the green, stretching branches
in praise. The cold sky is crisp and clean.
The little boy in me
wants to go out to play.

Little boy, where did you go?
Where are you now?

He's in the snowy air, head full
of toboggans, tea trays, sledging
down Primrose Hill, a smile
frozen on his face.

Now he stands under the limes
on the village green. Enjoy.
The trees know where you are,
but nobody else.

Pure Light

Snow sweeps over the turning tide
into Norfolk's curved back.
It settles on cliff tops, marshes,
papers the ground, and when the moon
drops its smudged thumbprint on the sea,
the only light is from land,

pure light, reflecting certainty
up into the dark ice-rink sky,
a clear disbelieving voice
when all around seems sacred.

Drifts scatter along the coastal path.
A group of daffodils,
brassy and leggy, flutter
at a paper boy,
but he wobbles away.
I clear the snow around them,
feel their glow of expectation.

No God

I still think there's no God,
but when I see the blond beach at Wells
stretch far out to sea,
enjoy the hug of darkness
as night falls from a giant sky
to wrap us in its closing light,
or see pink, red and crimson poppies,
our anxieties spilling in the wind,
the harvest of this place makes me wonder.

Roast Potatoes

Roast potatoes have their eccentricities
and like a friend or lover,
I don't like them perfect,
too fluffy, too mumsy in the middle.

I like my potatoes a little burnt,
a crisp crunch in the mouth.
I don't mind a chase round the plate,
some foreplay – but just a bit.

A heap of roast potatoes
is a kiss on the neck,
a frog, all heartbeat, sitting on a water lily leaf –
so much better than a pile of peas.

I like them on a Friday night
in my mouth, in my lap, in my hands,
I just love roast potatoes
any way at all.

Big Breakfast

My breakfasts are synonymous with me.
You couldn't say I was a bowl of fruit.
I don't like dieting or herbal tea.

I'm twelve stone ten and nearly fifty-three,
I'm thin on top and yet my bum's still cute.
My breakfasts are synonymous with me.

Grill me a chop, cook me a kedgeree
Give me my rifle and something to shoot.
I don't like dieting or herbal tea.

Braise me a steak, pour me a burgundy
with mushrooms on toast and salmon en croute.
My breakfasts are synonymous with me.

Fry me an egg, stir me a fricassée –
whisk me an omelette and I'll fill my boots.
I don't like dieting or herbal tea.

Don't make me eat a bowl of strawberries –
open the beer, we'll get as pissed as newts.
My breakfasts are synonymous with me.
I don't like dieting or herbal tea.

Ham and Eggs

I want to tell you something:
how I fell in love with ham and eggs,
a darling of food.
Like being in lust, I couldn't help touching,
wanted to go back for more and more.

I needed ham and eggs for breakfast,
for lunch, tea and supper, in bed
during the night
with bread, butter and beer.
I canoodled with ham in the pink,
off the bone, medium sliced with two eggs
silky and senseless on top.

One day my wife, who's not a bad cook,
said, "You have all the ham and eggs
you want. Devote yourself to ham and eggs.
I'm off. When you're cured, I'll return."

It was then life become an omelette,
a cheese one, gooey with Emmental.
I've forgotten about ham and eggs,
but the wife is still suspicious.

Lager

Lager is like a foreign country
and has its dialects.
Some are pale beaches,
others Moroccan sand, a drumbeat
or a quick headache.

I want to see the glass angled at my heart,
gold rising to the rim,
a patch of cloud settling at the top,
then feel cold shock in the cave of my mouth,
as light waves ribbon down,
brighten me inside.

I imagine John Mills in *Ice Cold in Alex*,
battling through the desert, seated
in that bar in Alexandria. I can see
him glazed at his glistening glass,
finger its perspiration,
lift the drink and say,
"Worth waiting for."

Strawberries and Cream

Norfolk cream is bright and brimming,
whipped sun and cloud, full of calories.
I want to sit, my head in the sky
in a warm cholesterol ssh of air, sometimes
lick my lips, imagine how sublime
I'd feel to be a strawberry:

Clotted cream spilling down my strawberry
head, sitting naked in a punnet, brimming
heat and expectation, a sublime
dream, bathing in a thousand calories.
And yet I think I'd tire, sometimes
want to be a raspberry mousse, fluffy in the sky.

I can't help staring at the Norfolk sky,
its face a fizzy glass of strawberry
blush, and when it sometimes
floods my nose, a shimmer brimming
effervescence, I think of kisses, love and calories,
my red socks – and feel sublime.

Sublime enough to write in capitals SUBLIME
in cloud, strewn about the sky.
No low-fat milk for me, only calories
rich and buttery, a strawberry

fool, a lush of cream, brimming
in the Norfolk air. And sometimes

if it rains champagne, let's hope it's sometimes
rosé, with a glacé cherry, just sublime.
My smile will be all wide and brimming,
a spirit of the alcoholic kind, and sky
will drop me in its tub of strawberry
ice, to sober me with calories.

I'd want to splash those calories
on my head, feel them trickle down, sometimes
sigh, and think how nice, how strawberry!
And when my wife, who after all is more sublime
than any bowl of cream or sunny clouds of sky,
finds me lying on my side, I'll blow her brimming

kisses, full of calories and love sublime,
and sometimes in the cream tea Norfolk sky
I'll see a strawberry smile, me all brimming.

Cheddar Cheese

This sunlit land,
not a piece of moon with moody
valleys and dark mountains,
I keep coming back to you.

The one I slice thick and thin,
grill on toast, grate on potatoes and bolognese,
queen – no – king of cheeses
I would lay my life down for you.

Would you do the same for me?

Sid's Café

Oasis of Lamb's Conduit Street.
I haven't been in for six months.
"Your usual, is it?" says the waitress.
It's as though I've just returned from war.
Her smile warms me
and she's remembered what I was eating – six months ago.
"Yes, please," I answer, "and a cup of tea…"
"Is that a lager as well?" she says, prompting.
"Well… er, no," I say, "I'll have the lager instead."

She brings my fried chicken and on top
a bonfire of spaghetti bolognese,
steaming like a sexy sonnet.

When it comes to pudding,
she doesn't ask about the trenches,
just offers today's crumble and the cup of tea.
I want to chat about how it's rained,
been raining for ever,
but she's off to clear a table.

The crumble is as guilty as a week's calories;
a pale liquid sun smoothes away the day.
When I leave, chairs are being stacked.
It's still raining. I haul on my coat,
I'm off to the front.

I Want To Be Buried In A Restaurant

close to Primrose Hill,
in the dining area, not deep down,
so I can hear what is being ordered,
the clink of drinks.

It must be a restaurant my children like,
not so cheap they come too often,
nor too ritzy they can't afford the bill.

They will be seated at a table
over me and I will listen
to the bubble and chat of their lives.

I don't want to hear problems, like:
the boiler pressure was too high
and the downstairs flat was flooded,
or my daughter's lost her Visa card —
for the third time this month —
and the roof is leaking, but just a bit.

I'd like to hear them enjoy a meal,
the purr of tidy conversation
as she eats a goat's cheese salad,
her partner pouring glasses of glugging wine.
I want to learn my son has paid off his loans,
doesn't mind wearing matching socks —
while I just lie there
a few inches below the floor.

After My Funeral

which may be as short
as you feel you can get
away with, please

go to my sheep,
the pretty ones grazing
on the bookshelf. Tell
them I am dead and find
someone who will
enjoy their company.

Serve alcohol, offer
egg and mayonnaise bridge rolls,
smoked salmon sandwiches,
all sprinkled with ground pepper.
I will like this a lot.

And to my wife and children,
"Thanks for the memories,"
these are now yours
to bring out now and again.
Enjoy them like a meal
in your favourite restaurant
with someone you care for.

Absence

If I talk to her, it's not a long conversation,
just quiet thoughts going out on the air,

and though I have the habit of answering for her,
I know it's my reply not hers.

I don't think it's wrong to speak her words.
I know she cannot answer, but if sometimes

the wish to talk brings her back to me,
who am I to argue it isn't her I hear?

Visiting

I took my children to see photographs
of their mother's past,
her fields of corn, wild grass, blown poppies.

After tea, their aunt asked them
"Have you enjoyed yourselves?"
I remember hearing those words long ago

when I went to tea with aunts.
"Yes, thank you," we answered smiling,
and for an instant we were all young again.

Menorah

The seven branches of the candelabrum
have withered; tarnished
silver no longer sparkles.

Under the base I turn the key
once again hear
the tune played at Chanukah.

It surprises me how that tinkerbell sound,
not heard since the death of my first wife,
still makes the silver sparkle.

Inheritance

I open the suitcase, the red one
stored in the loft, undo
its winding smile of a zip,
see crushed tissue folded over dresses
of Liberty prints and fabrics. I trail
my fingers over intricate sewing,
embroidered in flowers.

Some go back twenty years, others ten.
I place them on the bed, see
days of summer, parties and school,
an evening of lurex I couldn't wait
to get you out of.

I pick up a velvet dress, hold it close
to my face, then a blouse.
One day these will be our daughter's.

Walk on Hampstead Heath

Let's go for a walk.
I know I never ask;
but today I'd like to go to the Heath,
sit on the bench,
look at the grand spire of St Jude's,
its straight back
high in the horizon.

There you are, we're walking,
I haven't forgotten how —
one foot in front of the other.
I should do this more often,
but... I won't make an excuse,
you know them all.

The air is chilly,
but your hands are warm.
Here's the bench,
let's sit for a few moments.
How is it you always know
what I'm thinking?

Mrs Phillips

I said to Mrs Phillips that we weren't married anymore
and when she asked why
I said it's because she drinks white wine
and I drink red.

"Well, that's not a good enough reason,
and I'm not married to you either," she said.
"And why's that?"
"Because you don't eat greens or fruit
and you're turning into a pistachio nut."

So I kissed her. The sort of kiss
I save for certain moments,
the kiss that feels like an explosion of tiramisu
and I get excited, then short of breath.

"How's that?" I boasted.
"Not bad for a pistachio nut," she said.
And then I offered her a drink.

"Red or white wine?" I asked.

Worried

I have a lot in my head.
This is not unusual.

My wife tells me I mustn't think,
and if I must
I should think about fields, naked women,
champagne and bubble bath.

This is incredibly nice of her.

A Kiss a Day

"Give us a kiss," my wife said,
"and one for tomorrow,
and the next day
and the next."

After, when I smiled
she said, "That's a nice smile,
why not do that more often?"

Wedding Ceremony

A giggle of rabbis,
the weight of their faith so close
I can touch it. They join hands,
circle, clap a wedding song.
The dance is on everyone's face.

Love

Most think it will last for ever,
others wait for it to end.
A few decide it will never happen,
many hope and some pretend.

I Still ask My Children

if they've got money,
remembered their keys.

Grandfather used to fuss a lot,
bent to peer through
the car window, blew us a kiss
as he waved goodbye.

When my children leave,
I feel him inside me,
the lines on his forehead,
combed back grey hair.
I tell them to drive carefully,
not to touch the door handles,
don't choke on your sweets.

Hugs and Handshakes

They stopped when I started work, the hugs.
Each time we met or said goodbye
father shook my hand –
like a business colleague.

I didn't really notice, probably
thought I was old enough.
Maybe I was.
But when a hug becomes a handshake
something changes,
like the easiness of a lounge
becoming the formality of a drawing room.

Last week I went on holiday.
My son asked for a hug.
As he left for work I kissed his cheek.

Getting Older

Today the sky sang to the wind,
a dirge about the age our parents always were,
the age we never wanted for ourselves
as grandparents died
and we found love at discos or university.

The song dipped in and out of trees,
sun glinted on a TV aerial
and there they were: my daughter,
sparkling like tonic water,
son, cool as the cranberry juice he drinks.

Then a pigeon gusted about, tried
to land on a bare branch,
dithered too long, was blown sideways
against the pavement of the wind,
and the song grew louder,
first a lament, then a hymn, and a dream.

Fox Trap

Slumping snow covered his tracks.
He dragged a leg,
limped into his lair,
curled on a rug of leaves.

He smelt his blood,
a highwayman's blood, still heard
the clatter of the trap,
clamp of its teeth.

His legs had no go,
but he wanted tomorrow,
the rocks and crags of Hardwick Ridge,
chill of its streams,
to bite the warm neck of a rabbit.

He felt his bones lose grip,
flicker of breath.
Then he opened his eyes,
saw the white gauze air change
to a different shade of white.

Fox in the Garden

A fox's breath
cold on a conservatory window,
his tongue lolling pink
from his mouth.

I want to let him in,
hold a chunk of world
in my arms, feel his heart
against my chest.

He pants from a night raid,
drags the scrag of a blackbird,
shakes its head
till feathers scatter.

Now he's under the hawthorn,
eyes a sharp stare of arrowhead.
I guess what he wants,
stretch my hand to touch the glass.

He backs off,
turns towards himself,
leaves a shadow of shoulder,
a rustle of hedge. I feel

his wilderness, a trembling
of backyard animal.
In bed I turn and turn,
want winter on my face.

Suburban Fox

He would saunter to the park,
his shriek piercing my sleep
as he padded through his kingdom.

This morning he staggered,
head low, eyes darker.
Daffodils flagged a warm spot
where he sank,
his face pointing nowhere.

His tail was limp,
burnt by the late frost.

When the Council came
with a cardboard box,
a shield of crocuses
had poked through the grass,
flickering like gas lights,
protecting him from sight.

Christmas Fox

Eyes flicker amber in the gloom.
A vixen stands on the street edge
then sprints —
a dash of ginger punctuation
lighting up the beam of my headlamps:
russet coat, shiny tail, a blurred slipstream.

In three long seconds she crosses the tarmac
head aimed for the kerb's finishing line,
all limbs outstretched, a glow in the air
as she rises after every bound,
vanishes into a garden.

Dartmouth Park, London,
a late Christmas present.
I smile home, slink inside.

Stepping Off

...so I stepped from lawn to bare earth
to where the cypress had died,
into the den's darkness amongst the rusty
coats of foxes. No shock, just surprise
at the warmth of smoky breath.

That night I didn't think, *What if*, or *Should I?*
Just did it. Raided the fish bins at Corney's —
I felt like the first time I'd touched a naked breast —
swaggered down Finchley Road, licking
salt from my lips. Then seven miles under

the sky's dimly lit stars
to the zoo and its broth of smells.
I slept by the lake in the park
near the bridge to the gardens, woke when frost
fierce and fiery set me alight and the moon's

cold hands shivered me. I padded back.
Postmen grouched to work. Milk carts purred.
Inside the den, the others. I lay amongst them,
closed my ears to sparrows, the coughing cars.
Slept fifteen hours without waking. Went out to eat.

I don't think I can step back, not sure I'd want to.

Saying Goodbye

Victoria Station forecourt.
Young boys tread water
trying not to go under.

In we go, past the barrier
to the slam of closing carriage doors,
my hand held tight.

I climb in amongst the rabbits,
tuck boxes and other nine year olds.
Mother is on the platform smiling.

The window is drawn down,
hiss of steam letting off.
No one has drowned.

There's a jerk as the train pulls
me backwards to Eastbourne.
The smile on mother's face disappears.

Bath Time Butterflies
at Boarding School

A white butterfly comes to rest
on the edge of the bath, level with my eyes.
She's a Large White – I'd been praying
to see one soon – and her wings quiver
in the steamy heat of the water.
She flits to my stomach, settles between
my thighs. Then others fly in:
Red Admirals, Painted Ladies, more Large Whites,
a mass of wings fanning the glow
in a swirl of colour, till their flutter
giddies me in a breathless rainbow rush
and they're flying off to another fourteen year old boy.
It was better than scoring a penalty,
even mother sending money.
I tell myself I'll give up the butterflies
when I've seen them ten times,
but after I get to double figures, I lose count.

Ode to a Bra

Bra strap: shock of scarlet
crosses the pale prairie of a back.
Call me a C cup,
but I wish I was a bra,
a try-on bra in Marks & Spencer.

Oh, to hold in the round of my hands
the pleasures of the underwired,
to have some pretty lace,
tight elastic and a hidden fastener
for the fumbling.

Dear God, I know when we are dead
there is nothing,
but if you will bring me back
as a bra, if you do this,
I will never ask
to be a nightdress again.

Spanish Sighs

There's a sigh hanging over the mountain.
I can hear its breath,
and if I look along the ridge
where horizon meets rock,
there it rests, languid, almost hypnotic
and because I've never seen
a sigh before, all I want to do is look.

I've felt many creep up on me,
linger in my chest,
then felt a... swoosh as they undulate
past my larynx, out into the world.

But this is different.
My eyes cling to the top of the mountain
all craggy with trees.
It's as if the sigh is pleased
to be released in this place.

Perhaps this is where all the sighs go —
our troubles and contentments —
to the top of Spanish mountains to vaporise.

Then in the time it takes me
to wonder at the flavour of bougainvillea,
the sigh drifts off —
just glides away into the sky,
leaves me to stare,
slightly open-mouthed.

Ghost of a Roman General

Hadrian's Wall — 1939

I heard three Germans, saw them on the Wall.
They made me shiver, think about the past.
It was the way they stood straight-backed, and all
strode to and fro. So when one of them asked

which way was south I quickly pointed north,
and felt myself go red inside. They climbed
ahead and stomped away, waved to a fourth
who stood there pissing on the wall behind.

I travelled back towards the fort, went in
near the sign HQ, passed through the barracks.
There I paused and smelt latrines, remembering
the border raids, the barbarians' attacks.

Those days of Empire made me think of home.
Summer is warmer when you're back in Rome.

American Immigration

At passport control, Los Angeles airport,
I showed a bar of Cadbury's Fruit and Nut.

The immigration officer seemed perplexed
and asked again.

This time, after much fumbling,
I gave him a Crunchie bar and a smile.

My wife (who hates any embarrassment)
intervened, apologising for my English humour.

Instead of being sent to the back of the queue
as I expected, I was arrested.

So I took out a Hershey bar and stamped on it.
I'm writing this in prison. Please send more chocolate.

Hot Clematis

It's the water in the soil,
the deluge from winter's soaking,
that's turned this skimpy
smile of a flower into a sexual predator.

This year's clematis
have had hormone therapy.
They leer at me
and as I pass, they look me up and down.

The white ones stretch up my porch
bursting with weather.
I can feel their heat
and touch their petals.

Foxgloves

Bees bumble about,
knock into each other
to get at the mouths of foxgloves.

Last night the rain
rinsed orange rust from the clouds.
The warm sheet of sun is on my shoulders.

I want to ask those bees if the pollen
tastes alright, or is the flavour
different – just a little bitter this year?

The Melancholy of Cows

Cows seem to know about melancholy.
Maybe they've been branded with its syllables,
faint scars which redden
in the daylight of memory. Perhaps

they feel those ancient worlds, landscapes
etched white on their backs, geography
of the past weighing in their hearts.
Or have our daily expectations dredged

all light from them? But I can see into
their mournful spirits, know
that underneath the rough pasture
of thoughts there is a playful field.

How else could clotted cream, gloriously
soft and golden, look like a naked mistress?

Spotted

There's a squirrel busy in the hawthorn.
It jolts about on bare branches,
fur covered in a sheen of sleety rain.

Now it sits in a tremble,
fearful to be seen alive.
The tip of its tail,
where fur is thinnest, quivers.

I've stood in a room, been spotted
with a handful of peanuts in my fist,
fed them into my mouth
followed by a gulp of wine,
then started picking at the crisps
trying not to seem so naked.

Back outside, a pigeon heavy with age crashes
into the tree and the squirrel is gone,
an arc of grey in the damp air.

2060

for John

Last night we enjoyed a beer,
agreed to meet in the year 2060,
but I don't remember where.

Will it be a café in Golders Green
or Kentish Town? What if these places
don't exist and the map of North West
London has changed or a meteor
has sunk this city beneath the world?
I know I will recognize you —

you won't be looking distressed
as you trudge to chess or find a printer.
But what if we are dead, what then?

All I can say is, we should still go looking.
A deal's a deal.

Prayer

Prayer comes from a murmur in the heart –
reach of hand,
call of name,
son, daughter, lover.

Faith is a fragile thing –
a crocus trampled in the park
white petals crushed,
daffodils, stems broken in the wind.

Prayer is not just for believers.